ILLUSTRATED CLASSIC EDITIONS

The Adventures of Sherlock Holmes

A. Conan Doyle

adapted by
Malvina G. Vogel

Illustrations by
Brendan Lynch

BARONET BOOKS, New York, New York

WITHDRAWN

ILLUSTRATED CLASSIC EDITIONS

edited by
Malvina G. Vogel

Contents

About the Author

Arthur Conan Doyle was born in 1859 in Edinburgh, Scotland. He studied medicine, and in 1882 opened his practice. But patients did not flock to young Dr. Doyle too quickly, and during the long months of waiting for them, he began writing.

Although Doyle's first stories were not very successful, his first Sherlock Holmes novel, *A Study in Scarlet,* was an instant success. Doyle used one of his medical school teachers, Dr. Joseph Bell, as a model for Holmes. Bell was brilliant, not only at diagnosing the illnesses of his patients, but in studying their appearance, background, and habits to learn about them as well. These remarkable skills of observation and deduction Doyle transferred to Sherlock Holmes, so that the great detective is able to listen to the odd, mysterious, strange, and occasionally absurd stories his clients bring him, and make sense out of them.

Sherlock Holmes and his friend and assistant, Dr. John Watson, appear in 66 short stories and four novels by Arthur Conan Doyle. The three mystery thrillers you will read in this book are part of the collection of short stories which appear in *The Adventures of Sherlock Holmes.*

Once Holmes was established as a worldwide legend, Doyle himself came to be regarded as an expert crime solver. Real-life cases were brought to him, and he is credited with proving the innocence of many people unjustly imprisoned. Probably no other author has been able to create a fictional character who has become so real to his readers as Arthur Conan Doyle did with Sherlock Holmes.

Holmes Invites Watson In.

The Red-Headed League

As Dr. John Watson called on his friend, Mr. Sherlock Holmes, one autumn day, he found the great detective deep in conversation with a very stout, red-faced elderly gentleman, with fiery red hair.

"Forgive me, Holmes," said Watson in the doorway. "I didn't mean to intrude."

"Not at all," said Holmes. "Come in and close the door behind you." Then turning to his guest, the detective explained, "Dr. Watson has helped me solve many of my most successful cases, and I have no doubt that he will be just as useful in helping me solve yours too, Mr. Wilson."

The stout gentleman nodded at Dr. Watson as Sherlock Holmes sat back in his armchair, putting his fingertips together, as was his habit when he was in a thoughtful mood.

After Dr. Watson had seated himself on the sofa, Holmes leaned forward and spoke. "Mr. Jabez Wilson here has begun telling me a story which promises to be one of the most unusual I have heard in some time. I'm quite certain that a crime has been committed, but I want you to listen to the story from the beginning, Watson, right from Mr. Wilson's lips, and I'm sure you'll agree that I've never had a case like this before."

Jabez Wilson pulled a dirty, wrinkled newspaper from his pocket and flattened it on his knee. It was a page filled with classified ads. As Mr. Wilson ran his finger down one column, Watson took a few moments to study him, realizing full well how much he could

Jabez Wilson's Classified Ad

learn about the man from his appearance —
according to the methods Sherlock Holmes
had taught him.

Jabez Wilson's clothes revealed him to be
only an average British tradesman, although
the heavy vest chain with a piece of triangu-
lar metal hanging from it caught Watson's eye.
But other than that, there was nothing
remarkable about the man, except his blazing
red hair and his expression of anger.

Holmes noticed Watson studying their
guest, and he smiled. "Except for the fact that
Mr. Wilson has at some time done some manual labor," said Holmes, "that he has been in
China, and that he has done a great deal of
writing lately, I cannot discover anything
else."

Jabez Wilson looked up from his newspaper
with a start. "How in the name of heaven did
you know all that, Mr. Holmes?" he asked. "It's
true I once did manual labor. My first job was
as a ship's carpenter."

Holmes Knows Much About Wilson.

"Your hands, my dear sir," said Holmes. "Your right hand is much larger than your left, and the muscles are more developed."

"But the writing?" gasped Wilson.

"The right cuff on your jacket sleeve is shiny from rubbing along paper," explained Holmes, "and the patch on your left elbow is smooth where you rest it on the desk."

"Amazing!" cried Jabez Wilson. "But how did you know I had been in China?"

"The fish tattooed just above your right wrist could only have been done in China. I have made a thorough study of tattoos from around the world and can easily identify those from every country. And besides, the coin hanging from your watch chain is Chinese too."

"Well, I never!" said Jabez Wilson, laughing heartily.

"Now to the business at hand," said Holmes. "Have you found the advertisement, Mr. Wilson?"

Jabez Wilson's Right Hand.

THE RED-HEADED LEAGUE

"Yes, I have it now," he answered, with his thick red finger planted halfway down the newspaper column. "This is the ad that began it all. Just read it."

Watson took the paper Mr. Wilson reached out and began to read:

"TO THE RED-HEADED LEAGUE: ACCORDING TO THE TERMS OF THE WILL OF THE LATE EZEKIAH HOPKINS, OF LEBANON, PENNSYLVANIA, U.S.A., THE RED-HEADED LEAGUE WAS FORMED. NOW THERE IS ROOM FOR ONE MORE MEMBER OF THE LEAGUE WITH A SALARY OF 4 POUNDS A WEEK IN RETURN FOR VERY SIMPLE SERVICES. ALL RED-HEADED MEN WHO ARE IN GOOD HEALTH AND ABOVE THE AGE OF 21 ARE ELIGIBLE FOR MEMBERSHIP. APPLY IN PERSON MONDAY, AT 11:00 A.M., TO DUNCAN ROSS, AT THE LEAGUE'S OFFICE, 7 POPE'S COURT, FLEET STREET."

When Watson finished reading, he sat back, puzzled. "What on earth does this mean?" he asked.

Watson Reads the Ad.

Holmes chuckled. "A bit odd, isn't it?" he said. Then turning to Jabez Wilson, Holmes continued, "And now, sir, tell us about yourself, your household, and what has happened to you since you read this ad."

"Yes, Mr. Holmes," said Jabez Wilson. "Since the day that ad appeared in *The Morning Chronicle,* on April 27, 1890, only two months ago, my life has been strangely changed .... Well, to begin I have a small pawnbroker's shop on Coburg Square, here in London. It's not a very large business, and it just about provides me with a living. I used to have two assistants, but now I only keep one. It would have been hard enough to pay him, but he was willing to come and work for me at half-pay in order to learn the business."

"What is the name of this ambitious young man?" asked Holmes.

"Vincent Spaulding," replied Wilson, "and he's not such a young man either. It's hard to guess his age, but I couldn't ask for a smarter

16

Coburg Square

assistant. He surely could better himself and earn more than what I pay him, but he seems satisfied, so why should I give him any ideas?"

"You seem fortunate in having such an unusual assistant," said Holmes.

"Spaulding has his faults too," said Mr. Wilson. "Always with his hobby — photography. Snapping away with a camera, then diving down into the cellar to develop his pictures. But aside from this fault, on the whole, he's a good worker."

"He lives with you too?" asked Holmes.

"Yes, he and a woman who does simple cooking and cleaning. I am a widower, Mr. Holmes and never had a family. The three of us live very quietly.... Anyway, it was Spaulding who brought *The Chronicle* into my office just eight weeks ago today.

"Spaulding handed me the paper and said, 'I wish to God, Mr. Wilson, that I was a red-headed man!'

" 'Why's that?' I asked.

18

Spaulding Brought the Paper to Wilson.

" 'Because there's another vacancy in the League of Red-Headed Men,' he said eagerly. 'It's worth quite a fortune to any man who gets it. If my hair would only change color, I could probably be set for life.'

" 'What is this League, Spaulding?' I asked.

" 'Haven't you ever heard of the League of Red-Headed Men?' he said, surprised.

" 'Never!' I replied.

" 'That's odd,' he said, 'for you, yourself, are eligible to become a member.'

" 'And what does a member do?' I asked.

" 'Some slight work which doesn't interfere with his other occupation, and for it, he earns a couple of hundred pounds a year.'

"Well, Mr. Holmes, that made me prick up my ears, for, as I told you, business hasn't been all that good these last few years, and that extra couple of hundred pounds would come in handy. So I took the newspaper from Spaulding and read the ad. Then I asked him what he knew of this Red-Headed League.

"If My Hair Would Only Change Color...."

" 'Mr. Wilson,' he said, 'from what I know, the League was founded by an American millionaire, Ezekiah Hopkins, who was a bit peculiar in his ways. He, himself, was red-headed, and he had a great sympathy for all red-headed men. So, upon his death, his enormous fortune was left in the hands of trustees, with instructions to use the interest to help all red-headed men.'

" 'But there must be millions of red-headed men who would apply for membership in the League,' I told Spaulding.

" 'Not as many as you might think,' he answered. 'Old Hopkins was an Englishman by birth and has restricted membership in the League only to Londoners. Then, too, I hear that those with light red or dark red hair are rejected, and only those with real bright, blazing, fiery red hair are accepted. Anyone has only to walk in to apply, unless, of course, the few hundred pounds aren't that important to you.' "

Ezekiah Hopkins's Strange Will

THE RED-HEADED LEAGUE

"Of course you could qualify!" boomed Dr. Watson. "Your hair is red and rich enough to stand up under any competition."

"Yes, I thought so too, Dr. Watson," said Jabez Wilson, "so I had Spaulding close up the shop and come with me, since he seemed to know so much about the League."

"And when you got to the League's office?" asked Holmes.

"The sight that greeted us on Fleet Street was almost unbelievable. From every direction crowds of red-headed men filled the streets — men of every shade of red, from straw to orange to brick to liver. But there were not so many with real vivid, flame-colored red. When I saw the crowd waiting in Pope's Court, I was ready to give up in despair, but Spaulding wouldn't hear of it. Somehow, he managed to push his way through the crowd until he led me right up the steps to the office."

"A most interesting experience," said Holmes. "Do go on."

Pushing Through the Crowd in Pope's Court

"There was nothing in the office but a couple of wooden chairs and a card table, behind which sat a small man with a head even redder than mine. He spoke a few words to the men on line ahead of me and seemed to find fault with each one. When it came to my turn, he smiled at me and closed the door.

" 'This is Mr. Jabez Wilson,' said Spaulding. 'He wishes to fill the opening in the League.'

" 'He seems well suited for it,' said the man. 'I cannot recall ever seeing such a fine head of red hair.' Then he suddenly stepped toward me, shook my hand, and congratulated me.

"Then he dropped my hand and said, 'I hope, dear sir, that you will forgive me for what I am about to do, but I must make absolutely certain.' And he seized my hair in both his hands and tugged until I yelled with pain.

"When he finally let go, there were tears in my eyes, but he calmly explained, 'We have to be careful, for twice we have been deceived by

"He Seized My Hair and Tugged . . . ."

wigs, and once by paint.' Then he stepped over to the window and shouted at the top of his voice that the vacancy had been filled. A groan of disappointment came up from the crowd below, and they all began to troop away in different directions.

"Then the red-headed man turned to me and said, 'I am Duncan Ross of the League, and I'll need to ask some questions. First, are you a married man, and do you have a family?'

"When I told him no, his face fell.

" 'Dear me!' he said sadly. 'That is very serious indeed. The League is most anxious for its members to have children who can carry on their red hair.'

"My face dropped in disappointment, Mr. Holmes, but after several minutes, Ross said it would be all right — he would make an exception because he was so taken with my red hair. Then he asked when I'd be able to begin my duties with the League.

" 'But I already have a business,' I told him.

The Vacancy Had Been Filled.

" 'Oh, never mind about that, Mr. Wilson,' cried Vincent Spaulding. 'I'll look after that for you.'

" 'What would be the hours?' I asked Ross.

" 'You must be at this office from ten to two every day without leaving. If you set foot outside this building during your work time, you lose the job forever. Mr. Hopkins' will is very clear on that point.'

"That, Mr. Holmes, sounded quite good, for I conduct my pawnbroker's business mostly in the evening. Besides, I knew that Spaulding was a good man and would do just as he promised. So I agreed to the hours with Ross, then asked him the pay.

" 'Four pounds a week,' said Ross.

" 'And the work I'm to do?' I asked.

" 'You will copy the *Encyclopedia Britannica,* page by page. The first volume is in that closet. You must provide your own ink, pens, and paper, but we provide this table and chair. Can you start tomorrow?'

Jabez Wilson Continues His Story.

"I agreed, Mr. Holmes, and Spaulding and I returned home, both of us pleased with my good fortune. For several hours I was elated, then my spirits dropped, and I persuaded myself that this had to be some kind of a joke or fraud someone was playing on me. But I could not figure out why. It seemed unbelievable that anyone would make a will leaving all that money to people for doing something as simple as copying the *Encyclopedia Britannica*. But, with Spaulding's encouragement and my curiosity aroused, I set off for Pope's Court the next morning, carrying a penny bottle of ink, a quill pen, and seven sheets of paper.

"To my surprise, everything was ready, and Mr. Duncan Ross was there to see that I got right to work. He gave me the 'A' volume of the *Encyclopedia* and then left. But he dropped in from time to time to see that everything was all right. At two o'clock, he said good-bye and complimented me on the

The "A" volume of the *Encyclopedia*

number of pages I had written.

"This went on day after day, Mr. Holmes, and on Saturday, Mr. Ross came in and handed me four gold sovereigns for my week's work. This went on week after week for eight weeks, the only change being Ross stopped in less and less as I worked, until he stopped coming at all. Still, I didn't dare leave the office for fear of losing the job.

"During those eight weeks, I wrote about Abbots and Archery and Armor and Architecture, and was nearly ready for the 'B' volume when suddenly the whole business came to an end."

"To an end?" asked Holmes.

"Yes, sir, just this morning. I went to work as usual at 10 o'clock, but the office door was shut and locked. A little square of cardboard was nailed onto the door. Here it is."

Jabez Wilson held up the cardboard as Dr. Watson read, "THE RED-HEADED LEAGUE IS DISSOLVED. OCTOBER 9, 1890."

A Shocking Sign!

Holmes immediately burst out laughing.

"I can't see anything funny," cried Mr. Wilson, his face reddening almost to the color of his hair. "If you can't do anything better than laugh at me, I'll take my business elsewhere."

"No, no," cried Holmes, shoving Jabez Wilson back in the chair from which he had half-risen. "I wouldn't miss your case for the world. But you must admit yourself, there is something a little funny about it. But tell me, what did you do next?"

"I was shocked, sir. I didn't know what to do. I checked at the other offices in the court, but no one knew anything. Then I went to the landlord to inquire about Duncan Ross and the Red-Headed League, but the man said he had never heard of any such names.

" 'It's the gentleman at number 4,' I told him.

" 'Oh, the red-headed man?' he said. 'Why, his name is William Morris. He told me he was

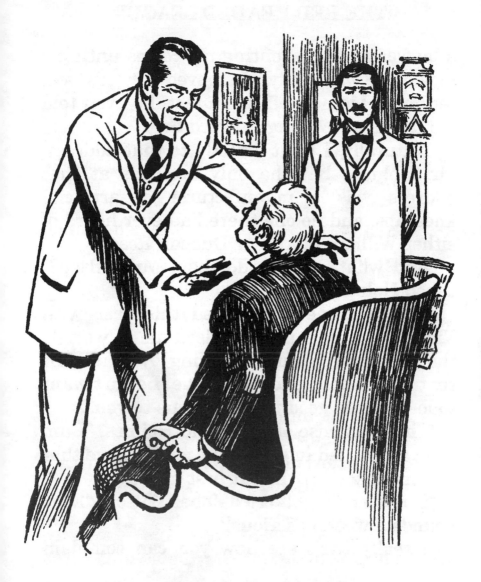

Holmes Bursts Out Laughing.

a lawyer and was renting my rooms until his new office was ready. He moved out only yesterday to his new office. In fact, he even told me it was at 17 King Edward St.'

"Naturally, I went directly to that address, Mr. Holmes, but the only business at that address was a manufacturer of artificial kneecaps, and no one there had ever heard of either William Morris or Duncan Ross."

"And what did you do then, Mr. Wilson?" asked Holmes.

"I went home and talked this over with Vincent Spaulding. He advised me to wait — that I'd surely hear something by mail. But that wasn't good enough for me. I didn't want to lose such a good job, so I came to you."

"That was wise of you," said Holmes. "I am most interested in your case, for I believe that it is more serious than it first appears."

"Serious enough!" cried Jabez Wilson. "Four pounds a week is serious!"

"I really can't see how you can complain

Tracking Down Duncan Ross

about the League," said Holmes. "After all, you are richer by over 30 pounds from it, to say nothing of the knowledge you have gained on every subject under the letter 'A'."

"But I do want to find out about them, Mr. Holmes — who they are and why they played this prank on me."

"We shall try to solve this mystery for you, Mr. Wilson," said Holmes, "but first, one or two questions. Your assistant, Spaulding — the fellow who first called your attention to the ad, how long had he been with you before this?"

"A month at the time of the ad."

"How did he come to you?"

"I advertised for an assistant — got a dozen applicants too."

"Why did you pick Spaulding?"

"He seemed bright and was willing to work cheap, as I told you."

"Yes, half-wages," muttered Holmes. "Tell me, Mr. Wilson, what does this Vincent

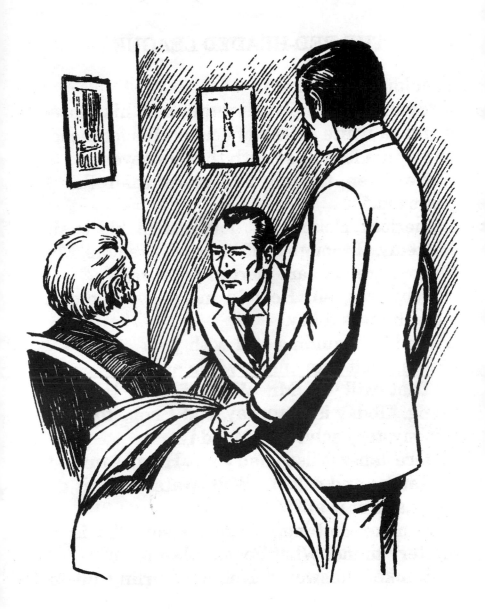

"We Shall Try To Solve This Mystery."

Spaulding look like?"

"Small, well built, very quick in his movements, a white splash of acid on his forehead, but with a face so smooth that he never has to shave, even though he's more than thirty years old."

Sherlock Holmes sat forward in his chair excitedly. "I thought so!" he cried. "Tell me, Mr. Wilson, are his ears pierced for earrings?"

"Why, yes, sir. He told me a gypsy did it when he was a boy."

"And is Spaulding still with you?"

"Yes. I left him only a while ago."

"That will do, Mr. Wilson," said Holmes, rising. "Today is Saturday, and I hope to have this mystery solved by Monday."

Once Jabez Wilson had gone, Holmes turned to Watson and asked, "Well, Watson, what do you make of it all?"

"I make nothing," said Watson. "It is a mystery to me. What do you plan to do?"

"Smoke," answered Holmes, curling up in

"Are His Ears Pierced for Earrings?"

his chair, with his knees drawn up to his hawklike nose, his eyes tightly closed, and his black clay pipe clamped between his teeth. "Please do not speak to me for fifty minutes."

After a while, when Watson was almost certain that Holmes had dropped off to sleep, the detective suddenly sprang out of his chair. "Watson," he cried, "can your patients spare you for a few hours? I'd like you to go to a concert with me this afternoon."

"I'm free today, of course, Holmes. But what about...?"

"Come, come!" snapped Holmes impatiently. "I want to stop in the city first."

Holmes and Watson traveled by the underground and then on foot to Coburg Square, where Jabez Wilson had his business. The Square was formed by lines of dingy two-storied brick houses, which looked out onto a lawn of weedy grass and a few clumps of bushes. On a corner house, three gold balls and a brown sign with "JABEZ WILSON" in white

Visiting Jabez Wilson's Business

letters identified the pawnbroker's shop.

Holmes stopped in front of the building and looked it over, his eyes shining brightly. Then he walked slowly up the street and then down again to the corner, still looking intently at the houses. When he returned to the front of Wilson's house, he thumped vigorously on the pavement with his walking stick. Then he went to the door and knocked.

The door was opened by a bright-looking, clean-shaven young fellow who invited Holmes and Watson in.

"Thank you," said Holmes. "I only wanted to ask directions to the Strand."

"Third right, then fourth left," said Spaulding, and he quickly closed the door.

"Smart fellow, he is," said Holmes as he and Watson walked slowly away. "He is, in fact, the fourth smartest man in London. And as for daring, I'd say third. I've heard of Vincent Spaulding before."

"Then he has something to do with the Red-

Spaulding Gives Holmes Directions.

Headed League?" asked Watson.

"Yes."

"And you asked directions of him merely to see what he looked like?"

"Not *him,*" said Holmes, "rather the knees of his trousers. And I saw exactly what I expected to see."

"And why did you tap on the pavement?"

"That will come later, my dear Watson. For now, I wish to explore the streets behind Coburg Square."

As Holmes and Watson slowly walked past the buildings behind Jabez Wilson's shop, the street changed quickly. From the shabby, quiet Coburg Square, the street became one of the city's main traffic roads — with carriages and pedestrians hurrying in both directions. As they walked, Holmes called out the names of the shops and businesses they passed.

"Mortimer's Tobacco Shop, the Vegetarian Restaurant, the City and Suburban Bank, and McFarlane's Carriage Station office. And now,

Holmes Names the Businesses They Pass.

Watson, that does it. We're ready for lunch, and then off to our violin concert, where there are no red-headed clients to bother us."

That afternoon, Sherlock Holmes and Dr. Watson sat in St. James Concert Hall, with the great detective — himself a talented musician and composer — waving his long, thin fingers in time to the music. When the concert was over and Holmes and Watson were leaving the hall, Holmes finally brought up Jabez Wilson's case again.

"I believe, Watson, that a serious crime is being planned, but I feel that we have a chance of stopping it. Today being Saturday might complicate matters, but I shall need your help. Just be at Baker Street at ten tonight and kindly bring your army revolver." With a wave of his hand, Holmes turned on his heel and disappeared into the crowd.

Watson stood outside the concert hall for several minutes, bewildered. "What kind of stupid dolt am I?" he muttered to himself. "I

Enjoying the Concert

have seen and heard everything that Holmes has seen and heard, yet *he* seems to know exactly what has happened and what is about to happen, while I am completely confused."

As he rode home in a cab, Watson tried to puzzle it all out, but other than Holmes's hint that Vincent Spaulding, the pawnbroker's assistant, was a shrewd and dangerous man, Watson could figure out nothing.

Dr. Watson left his home at 9:15. Arriving at 221B Baker Street, he saw two hansom cabs standing at the door of the detective's home.

As Watson entered the house, he found Sherlock Holmes deep in conversation with two men. Watson recognized one as Peter Jones, a police inspector from Scotland Yard, but the other man, a tall, thin man with a long, dark coat and shiny hat, was a stranger.

"Aha! Our party is complete," said Holmes, as Watson entered. "My dear Watson, you know Mr. Jones of Scotland Yard."

Jones and Watson smiled and shook hands.

Watson Greets Inspector Jones.

"And let me introduce you, Watson, to Mr. Merryweather, who will be our companion in tonight's adventure." As he spoke, Holmes was buttoning up his pea jacket and taking his heavy hunting crop from the rack.

"I hope this does not wind up as a wild goose chase," said Mr. Merryweather gloomily.

"You can have confidence in Sherlock Holmes," said Inspector Jones. "His ways may be a bit unusual, sir, but he is most often quicker and more successful at solving cases than our police force."

"All right, Inspector Jones," said Mr. Merryweather, "if you say so. Still, I must confess that I shall miss my card game at my club. It's the first Saturday night in twenty-seven years that I shall not be there."

"I think you will find yourself playing for higher stakes tonight than you have ever played for before," said Holmes, "and that play will be more exciting. For you, Mr. Merryweather, the stakes will be 30,000

"You Can Have Confidence in Holmes."

pounds, and for you, Inspector Jones, the stakes will be a criminal you have been seeking for years."

"That is so, Mr. Holmes," said Inspector Jones. "For years, I have been following the trail of John Clay — the murderer, thief, and forger, but with no luck. He's a young man, but he is at the top in his profession. A pity too, for his grandfather was a royal duke, and young Clay has been to Eton and Oxford, two of England's finest schools. His brain is as cunning as his fingers, and I've never even managed to set eyes on him."

"Then I hope I shall have the pleasure of introducing you to Mr. John Clay tonight," said Holmes. "And now, Inspector, it is time to leave. If you and Mr. Merryweather will ride in the first hansom cab, Watson and I will follow in the second."

During the drive along London's gaslit streets, Sherlock Holmes sat humming the music he had heard that afternoon. Finally,

Following the Trail of a Murderer

Watson could contain himself no longer and he burst out, "Holmes, where are we going, and why are Inspector Jones and that Mr. Merryweather, whoever he is, going with us?"

"My dear Watson, we are very close now. This fellow Merryweather is a bank director, and so, personally interested in this matter. As for Jones, even though he's an absolute imbecile as a policeman, he's as brave as a bulldog and never lets go of his victim once he's captured him....Ah, here we are, and they are waiting for us."

The cab stopped on the street around the corner from Jabez Wilson's pawnbroker's shop, and Holmes, Watson, and Inspector Jones followed Mr. Merryweather down a narrow alley and through a side door, which he unlocked for them. They walked through a small corridor until a massive iron gate stopped them. Mr. Merryweather opened this, too, with a key and led the three men down a flight of winding stone steps.

Merryweather Unlocks a Side Door.

Mr. Merryweather stopped to light a lantern, revealing another iron gate. He unlocked this too, and the four men entered a huge cellar, piled high with crates and huge boxes.

"This vault cannot be reached from above," said Holmes, as he took the lantern and studied the cellar room.

"Nor from below," said Mr. Merryweather, striking his stick on the flagstones lining the floor. Then he gasped and looked up in surprise. "Wh-why, it sounds hollow! "

"You'll have to be quiet," said Holmes severely. "Any noise can ruin the success of my plan. Now please, Mr. Merryweather, sit down on one of the crates and try not to interfere."

The banker, looking a bit hurt, perched himself on a crate while Holmes fell to his knees and, with the lantern and magnifying glass, began to examine the cracks between the stones. After a few seconds, he sprang to

Holmes Examines the Stone Floor.

his feet and put the glass in his pocket.

"We have an hour to wait," said Holmes, "for they won't do anything until the good pawnbroker is in bed. Then they will get to work." Turning to Watson, Holmes added, "And now, Watson, as you have probably guessed, we are in the cellar of one of the major London banks. Mr. Merryweather is the chairman of the directors of that bank, so I'll let him explain to you why these daring criminals are so interested in this cellar right now."

"It's our French gold," whispered Mr. Merryweather. "We were warned that an attempt might be made to steal it."

"French gold?" asked Watson, puzzled.

"Yes. Some months ago, to strengthen our bank's resources, we borrowed 30,000 pounds in gold from the Bank of France. We never had the need to unpack the money, so it is still lying in these crates in the cellar."

"And now," said Holmes, "we must arrange our plans. First, Mr. Merryweather, we must

Gold from the Bank of France

darken the lantern. We cannot risk a light. Next, we must choose our positions. These are daring men who will not think twice about harming us, so we must be careful. I shall stand behind this crate, and the rest of you are to conceal yourselves behind some others. As soon as I flash a light on the criminals, close in and attack. If they fire, Watson, shoot them down!"

Watson cocked his revolver and placed it on the crate behind which he was crouching. As soon as the others were in place, Holmes slid the plate across the front of his lantern and left everyone in pitch darkness.

"They can retreat in only one direction," Holmes whispered to Watson. "That is through Mr. Wilson's house. But Inspector Jones has three officers waiting at the front door.... And now, we must be silent and wait."

As an hour went by, then an hour and a quarter, Watson's legs grew stiff, for he was

Waiting and Whispering in the Darkness

afraid to change his position. Suddenly, a glint of light sparkled on the stone floor. It lengthened into a yellow line. Then, without a sound, the opening widened and a hand appeared — a white, almost womanly hand. Its fingers felt around the stone floor, then quickly disappeared, and everything went dark again, except for one spark between the stones.

A moment later, one of the broad flagstones turned over on its side with a smashing sound. Over the edge peeped a clean-cut, boyish face which looked carefully about. Then, with a hand on either side of the opening, the fellow lifted himself up and out of the hole. Reaching back in, he lifted out a small, agile companion with a pale face and a head full of very red hair.

"It's all clear," whispered the first man. "Bring up the chisel and the bags and.... Great Scott! Jump, Archie! Get away while I hold them off!"

"It's All Clear."

Sherlock Holmes had sprung from behind a crate and grabbed the first young man by the collar. The other dived back into the hole, avoiding the clutch of Inspector Jones, who was left with only a torn piece of cloth from the man's coat in his hands.

The first man, John Clay, tried to pull out his revolver, but Holmes's hunting crop came down on his wrist, and the pistol clinked to the floor.

"It's no use, John Clay," said Holmes. "You cannot escape."

"So I see," answered Clay, "but at least my pal got away."

"But you're wrong!" cried Holmes. "There are three men waiting for him at the door to Mr. Wilson's house."

"You seem to have thought of everything. I must compliment you," said Clay.

"And I must compliment you too, John Clay, or Vincent Spaulding," said Holmes. "Your red-headed idea was quite ingenious."

Capturing John Clay

Inspector Jones reached for Clay's wrists and locked them together with a pair of handcuffs.

"Do not touch me with your filthy hands!" said Clay coldly. "I have royal blood in my veins, and I wish to be addressed as 'sir' and with the word 'please.'"

"Ha!" cried Jones with a sneer. "Well, will you please, sir, march upstairs where we can place your highness in a royal cab and take you to the police station."

"That's better," said Clay with a bow, and he walked off with the police inspector.

Mr. Merryweather turned to Sherlock Holmes and said, "Really, Mr. Holmes, I don't know how the bank can repay you."

"Just cover my expenses, Mr. Merryweather," said Holmes. "I've had one or two little scores of my own to settle with Mr. John Clay, and it has been a unique and remarkable experience, matching wits with the Red-Headed League."

"March Upstairs."

THE RED-HEADED LEAGUE

Later, in the early hours of the morning, as Holmes and Watson sat over a glass of whiskey and soda in Holmes's sitting-room, the detective explained, "You see, Watson, it was obvious from the start that the only possible purpose of the League's newspaper advertisement and the copying of the *Encyclopedia* was to get Jabez Wilson out of his pawnshop for several hours each day. The method probably occurred to Clay by his accomplice's red hair and Jabez Wilson's red hair. Surely, paying the not-too-bright pawnbroker four pounds a week was nothing when they stood to gain 30,000 pounds. John Clay's partner rented the temporary office as Duncan Ross, or William Morris, while Clay, himself, as Vincent Spaulding, urged Jabez Wilson to answer the League's advertisement."

"And that way, they made certain that Jabez Wilson was out every morning, giving them time to dig," added Watson. "But tell me, Holmes, what first made you suspicious?"

Holmes Explains How He Solved the Case.

"When I first heard that Vincent Spaulding had agreed to work for Mr. Wilson at half-pay, I figured he had a strong motive for getting the job."

"But how did you guess the motive?"

"I immediately ruled out robbery of Wilson's home or pawnshop, for there was nothing of great value for these criminals to make such elaborate plans and spend the money they did. So I decided it must be something out of the house. But what? Then I remembered Wilson's telling us of Spaulding's interest in photography and of his frequent disappearances into the cellar. Yes, Watson, the cellar was the clue! Vincent Spaulding had to be doing something in the cellar — something which took many hours each day for months. The only thing I could come up with was that he was digging a tunnel to some other building."

"And how did you make sure, Holmes?"

"When we first visited Coburg Square, I

Recalling Spaulding's Interest in Photography

tapped my walking stick on the pavement in front of Jabez Wilson's pawnshop."

"To see if the cellar was in front or in back," added Watson, pleased now to understand the great detective.

"Yes, Watson, and it was not in front. Then I rang the bell and, as I hoped, Spaulding answered it. I had come up against him in cases before, but we had never met face to face. Besides, it wasn't his face I looked at when he opened the door — it was his knees."

"Aha!" cried Watson. "Those wrinkled, dirt-stained, worn pants' knees told you that he had been on his hands and knees digging."

"Yes, and the only remaining question was what they were tunneling for. So, Watson, after we left Vincent Spaulding, we walked around the corner, and I observed the shops. When I realized that the City and Suburban Bank backed up against Jabez Wilson's shop, I knew I had the answer."

"And the business you had to take care of

Spaulding Had Been Digging.

after the concert?" asked Watson.

"I went to Scotland Yard and, with Inspector Jones, called upon Mr. Merryweather."

"And how could you be sure that Spaulding, or Gray, would attempt the robbery tonight?"

"When they closed the office of the Red-Headed League, that was a sign that they no longer had to keep Mr. Jabez Wilson out of the house. In other words, the tunnel was finished. They had to use it quickly, for it might be discovered, or the gold might be removed to another bank. Saturday would be good, for it would give them a full day on Sunday to make their escape before the bank opened on Monday. That's how I reasoned they would attempt the robbery tonight."

"Amazing, Holmes! You reasoned it out beautifully!"

"Ah, well, Watson," said Holmes with a yawn, "it saved me from boredom. But now I shall have to be bored until the next case comes along to challenge my wits."

Boredom While Awaiting a New Case

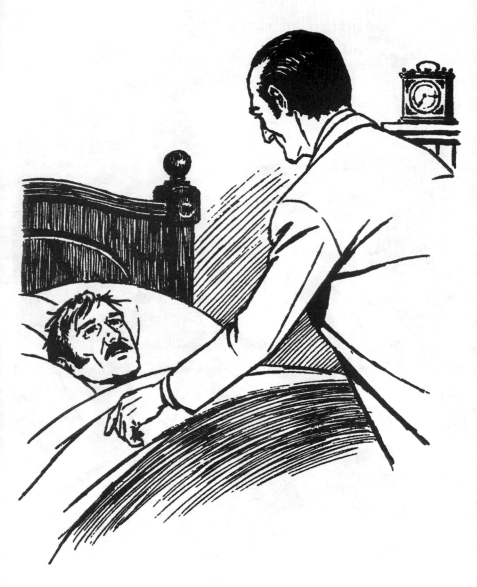

"Sorry to Wake You, Watson."

The Adventure of the Speckled Band

It was early in April in the year 1883 when Sherlock Holmes and his assistant, Dr. John Watson, were sharing Holmes's bachelor apartment at 221B Baker Street that the good doctor awoke one morning to find the great detective standing, fully dressed, by the side of his bed. As a rule, Holmes was a late riser, so Watson blinked in surprise to notice the clock on the mantel showing only 7:15 A.M.

"Sorry to wake you, Watson," said Holmes, "but Mrs. Hudson was awakened, she woke me, and I'm waking you."

"And just why did our good housekeeper wake you?" asked Watson.

"It seems a client has arrived — a young lady who is quite excited and insists on seeing me immediately. She is waiting in the sitting-room. When a young lady is up and about London at this hour, waking people out of their beds, I conclude that she has an urgent problem to discuss. I thought that if it proved to be an interesting case, you'd want to be in on it from the start."

"My dear Holmes, I wouldn't miss it for anything," cried Watson, as he jumped out of bed and threw on his clothes. "My greatest pleasure is following your investigation and admiring your rapid and logical deductions."

A few minutes later, Sherlock Holmes and Dr. Watson opened the door of the sitting-room. A lady, dressed in black and heavily veiled, rose from her seat near the window.

"Good morning, madam," said Holmes cheerily. "I am Sherlock Holmes, and this is

A Lady in Holmes's Sitting—Room

my friend and assistant, Dr. Watson. You may feel as free to speak in front of him as with me. Please, let us sit near the fire, which Mrs. Hudson has had the good sense to light. I see, madam, that you are shivering. I shall order you a cup of hot coffee."

"It is not the cold that is making me shiver," said the woman softly, as she moved nearer the fire. "It is fear, Mr. Holmes."

As she spoke, she raised her veil, revealing a pale, drawn face with frightened eyes, like those of a hunted animal. She appeared to be no more than thirty years old, but her dark hair was already streaked with gray, and her expression was weary and haggard.

"You must not be afraid," said Holmes soothingly, patting her hand. "We shall help you. Ah, I see you have come in by train this morning."

"But how could you know that?" she asked. "Did you see me at the station?"

"No, madam," answered Holmes, "but I see

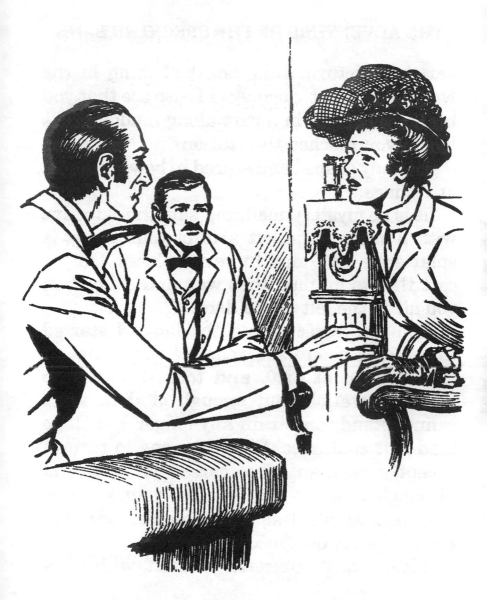

"You Must Not Be Afraid."

part of a return train ticket sticking in the wrist of your left glove. And I also see that you had a long drive in a cart along muddy roads before you reached the station."

The lady gasped and stared in bewilderment at Holmes.

"It is no mystery, madam," said the detective with a smile. "The left arm of your jacket is splattered with mud in seven places. Only a cart throws up mud that way and only when you sit to the left of the driver."

"You are correct," said the lady. "I started from home before six, reached the village of Leatherhead at 6:20, and took the train to Waterloo station. But enough of that, sir. I cannot stand this strain any longer. I shall go mad if it continues. I have no one to turn to except one man who cares for me, and although I cannot pay you for your services now, in a month I shall be married and will then have my own income."

"Please don't concern yourself with pay-

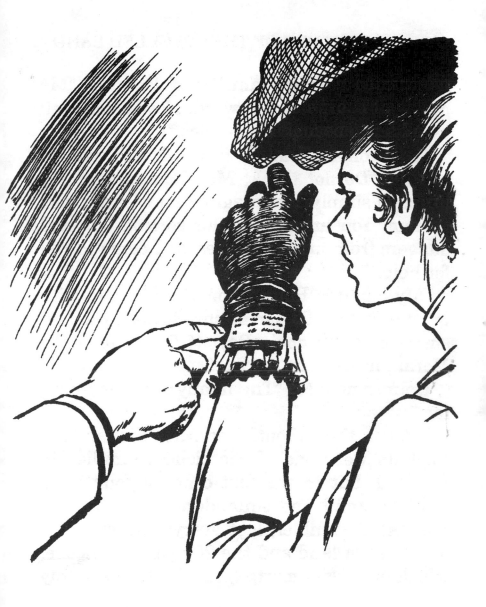

Holmes Spots the Woman's Train Ticket.

ment, my dear madam," said Holmes, "My profession is its own reward. Now please tell us how we might be of service."

The woman leaned forward and smiled weakly. "Do not think, Mr. Holmes, that my terror is simply the imagination of a nervous woman. You are famous for sorting out real dangers from imagined ones, so I came to you for help.

"My name is Helen Stoner, and I live with my stepfather, Dr. Grimesby Roylott, the last survivor of the noble Roylott family of Stoke Moran, in western Surrey."

Holmes nodded. "The family name is familiar."

"At one time," continued Miss Stoner, "the Roylotts were one of the richest families in England, but in the last century, four heirs were wasteful and squanderers, and finally, the last, a gambler, lost everything except a few acres of land and the 200-year-old house, which is heavily mortgaged. His only son, my

Dr. Grimesby Roylott

stepfather, realized that he would have to earn his own living, so with money borrowed from a relative, he went to medical school and established a large and successful practice in Calcutta, India. However, this was brought to an abrupt end when Dr. Roylott suspected his native butler of robbing him and beat the man to death. The doctor was imprisoned for many years and returned to England a defeated and depressed man.

"However, during his stay in India, Dr. Roylott married my mother, Mrs. Stoner, the young widow of a British army officer serving there. My twin sister Julia and I were only two years old at the time. Mother had a very comfortable income — more than 1,000 pounds a year — and in her will, she left that sum to Dr. Roylott, as long as Julia and I lived with him. However, when Julia and I married, part of that 1,000 pounds would go to each of us. The will took effect eight years ago, shortly after our return to England when my mother

Happier Times in India

was killed in a railway accident.

"We left London after her death, and Dr. Roylott took Julia and me to live with him in his old family house at Stoke Moran. The money my mother had left us was enough for all our wants.

"But a terrible change came over my stepfather about this time. Despite the joyous welcomes of all his old friends and neighbors, Dr. Roylott shut himself up in the old house and came out only to quarrel with anyone who came near the place. Violent tempers seem to have been inherited in the men of the Roylott family, and in my stepfather's case these led to several brawls, which ended in court. The local people then took to running from him, not only because of his uncontrollable anger, but because of his immense strength as well.

"Last week, he hurled the local blacksmith over a wall into a stream, and it was only by paying over all the money I could gather that I kept him out of court. His only friends seem

A Friendly Welcome at Stoke Moran

to be herds of wandering gypsies, who are allowed to camp on the estate. In return, they let him travel with them, sometimes for weeks at a time.

"He also has a passion for Indian animals and from time to time, several are sent over from India. Right now, he has a cheetah and baboon wandering freely over the grounds of the estate. The villagers fear these animals as much as they fear my stepfather.

"You can see, Mr. Holmes, that my poor sister Julia and I did not have happy lives. No servants would work for Dr. Roylott, and we cared for the big house ourselves. Julia was only thirty when she died two years ago, but her hair had already begun to whiten just as mine is doing."

"How did your sister die?" asked Holmes.

"Strangely, I fear, Mr. Holmes. You can well understand that living the life I describe Julia and I had no friends our age. However my mother had a sister, Miss Honoria Westphail,

Dr. Roylott's Pets

and Dr. Roylott permitted us to visit her occasionally. Two years ago, during a Christmas visit Julia and I made there, Julia met a naval officer. They soon fell in love and became engaged. When I returned to Stoke Moran and told my stepfather of her plans, he did not object. But two weeks before her wedding day, a terrible thing happened."

"Please, Miss Stoner, give me the exact details," said Holmes.

"I can do that easily," replied the woman, "for every moment of that dreadful time is very clear in my memory. Let me begin by explaining that the manor house is very old, and we occupy only one wing. The bedrooms are on the ground floor — the first is Dr. Roylott's, the second my sister's, and the third my own. There are no doors connecting them, but they all open into the same corridor."

"And the windows of these rooms?" asked Holmes.

"They face a large lawn. That horrible night,

Julia's Engagement

Dr. Roylott had gone to his room early, but Julia knew he wasn't asleep for she smelled his strong Indian cigars. Annoyed by the smoke, she left her room and came into mine, where we sat chatting about the wedding. At eleven o'clock, she got up to leave, but at the door, she paused and looked at me curiously.

" 'Tell me, Helen,' she said, 'have you ever heard anyone whistle during the night?'

" 'Never,' I said. 'Why?'

" 'During the last few nights, about three in the morning, a low, clear whistle wakened me. I couldn't tell where it came from — perhaps the next room, father's room, or perhaps the lawn.'

" 'It was probably those wretched gypsies,' I said, trying to explain it away.

" 'Then why didn't you hear it too, Helen?'

" 'Remember, Julia, I'm a heavy sleeper, and you are a light one.'

" 'I'm sure it was nothing,' she said with a smile as she closed my door. And a few

Troubled About a Strange Whistle

minutes later, I heard her turn the key in her lock."

"Did you and Julia always lock your bedroom doors at night?" asked Holmes.

"Always," replied Miss Stoner. "With the doctor's cheetah and baboon running loose, Julia and I felt safer that way."

"Of course, of course. Please go on," urged Holmes.

"I couldn't sleep that night — it was almost as if I had a feeling that something terrible was about to happen. It was a stormy night — the wind howling and the rain beating against the windows. Suddenly, amid the noise of the storm, I heard the wild scream of a terrified woman — it was my sister's voice.

"I sprang from my bed, wrapped a shawl around me, and rushed into the corridor. As I opened my door, I heard a low whistle, like the one Julia had described, and a few moments later I heard a clanging sound, as if some heavy metal had fallen. I ran to my sister's

"I Sprang from My Bed . . . ."

door and found it unlocked and swinging on its hinges, with Julia clinging to it and swaying, almost like a drunkard. Her face was white with terror, her hands groped towards me for help. As I caught her in my arms, her knees gave way and she fell to the ground, writhing and convulsing in pain. I bent over her and she suddenly shrieked out, 'Oh, my God! Helen! It was the band! The speckled band!' She lifted her hand weakly and pointed to Dr. Roylott's room. Then another convulsion seized her.

"I rushed out, calling loudly for my step-father, and met him as he opened his door in his dressing gown. When he reached Julia's side, she was unconscious. Even though Dr. Roylott sent for a doctor from the village, Julia died without ever regaining consciousness," she concluded with a sigh.

"Miss Stoner, are you certain about the whistle and the clanging metal sound?" asked Holmes.

"I could have sworn I heard it, but perhaps

"She Pointed to Dr. Roylott's Room."

the storm played tricks on me."

"Was your sister dressed?" asked Holmes.

"No, she was in her nightgown," said Miss Stoner, "but she was holding a box of matches in her left hand and the charred stump of a match in her right."

"That means she was trying to light a lamp when she became frightened. Tell me, Miss Stoner, did the coroner investigate your sister's death?"

"Very carefully, Mr. Holmes, especially since my stepfather's behavior had been strange. But the coroner couldn't discover any cause of death. Julia's door had been locked from the inside, and her windows had bars and shutters. The walls and floors were examined and found perfectly solid. The chimney is wide, but it is barred as well. No, Mr. Holmes, it seems certain that my sister was alone when she met her death."

"Were there no marks of violence on her?" asked Holmes.

Investigating Julia Stoner's Death

"None."

"Signs of poison?" asked Dr. Watson.

"The doctor examined her, but found nothing."

"And what do you think she died of?" asked Holmes.

"Pure fear — a terrifying shock. But I have no idea what frightened her."

"Were gypies camped on the estate at the time?"

"Yes."

"And what did she mean when she referred to a band — a speckled band?"

Helen Stoner looked puzzled. "At first, Mr. Holmes, I thought Julia was just delirious, then I thought perhaps she meant a band of people — the gypsies, maybe. They do wear spotted handkerchiefs on their heads, so Julia might have been referring to that."

Holmes shook his head. "I'm not satisfied. This all goes much deeper, Miss Stoner. But please go on."

A Gypsy Camp at Stoke Moran

"All that happened two years ago, and my life has been lonelier than ever — until lately. About a month ago, Percy Armitage, a dear old friend whom I have known for many years, asked me to marry him. My stepfather did not object, and we are planning a spring wedding."

"Then it seems you are about to begin a happier part of your life," said Dr. Watson.

"That's what I believed. But two days ago, my stepfather had some workers in to start repairs on our wing of the house. My bedroom wall had been opened up, so I had to move into the room in which my sister had died and sleep in her very bed. Last night as I lay there thinking of her terrible death, I suddenly heard a low whistle — the very same whistle Julia had described to me — the whistle that announced her death.

"I jumped up and lit the lamp, but saw nothing. I was too shaken to return to bed, so I got dressed and sat there waiting for daylight.

Shaken by the Strange Whistle

"When it came, I slipped out, hired a cart at a nearby inn, and drove to Leatherhead. There I boarded the train to London — and you."

"That was wise of you," said Holmes. "But you haven't told me everything."

"But I have!" exclaimed the woman.

"You are shielding your stepfather, Miss Stoner," cried Holmes as he leaped up and pushed back the lace frill of the woman's sleeve cuff. Five little red marks, the marks of four fingers and a thumb, were printed on the white wrist.

Helen Stoner immediately covered her injured wrist. "Dr. Roylott is a strong man," she said. "Perhaps he doesn't even know his own strength."

Sherlock Holmes was silent for several minutes as he leaned his chin on his hands and stared into the fire. Finally he spoke. "There are a thousand details I need to know, Miss Stoner, and we haven't a moment to lose. I must come to Stoke Moran today and examine

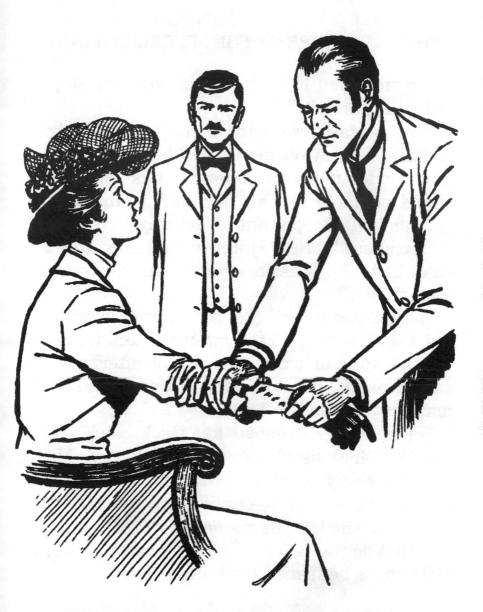

Holmes Finds Marks on Helen's Wrist.

the rooms. Can it be done without your step-father knowing it?"

"I'm certain we can arrange that, Mr. Holmes. Dr. Roylott mentioned he was coming into London today on important business that would probably last all day, and I can easily get our housekeeper out of the way."

"Excellent!" cried Holmes. "Watson and I shall be there. What are your plans for today, Miss Stoner?"

"I have two errands to take care of in town, but I shall return on the twelve o'clock train."

"And we shall arrive early in the afternoon," said Holmes. "I, too, have some business matters to attend to."

Helen Stoner dropped her thick black veil over her face as she rose. "Thank you, Mr. Holmes, and you too, Dr. Watson. My heart is lightened since I have confided my troubles to you." And she left the room.

"What do you make of it all, Watson?" asked Holmes, as he leaned back in his chair.

Thanking Holmes and Watson

"A dark and sinister business," answered Watson.

"Yet if Miss Stoner is correct in saying that the bedroom's floor and walls are solid and that no one could have entered through the door, windows, or chimney, then her sister must have been alone when she met her mysterious end."

"But what of those whistles and the strange words of the dying woman — a speckled band?" asked Watson.

"I don't know," said Holmes.

"Well, we know that the gypsies were on the grounds and they were friends of Dr. Roylott, and we could guess that the doctor wanted to prevent his stepdaughter's marriage. Perhaps he had them frighten her, and the metallic clang might have been caused by the gypsies at the shutters."

"I don't quite agree, Watson, and that is why we are going to Stoke Moran today.... But what's that noise ... and what the devil!"

Puzzling Over a Dark and Sinister Business

The door suddenly burst open and a huge man stood framed there. He was so tall that his hat brushed the top of the door frame, and so broad that he seemed to cover the opening from side to side. His clothes were an odd mixture of a professional man and a country man, with a black top hat, a long frock coat, and a pair of high gaiters. A hunting crop swung in his hand. His large, wrinkled face was yellowed from the sun as he looked at Holmes and Watson with an evil stare. His deep-set, bloodshot eyes and his high, thin nose made him resemble a vulture!

"Which of you is Holmes?" cried the man.

"It is my name, sir," answered the detective quietly. "But who are you?"

"Dr. Grimesby Roylott of Stoke Moran," answered the man.

"Indeed, Doctor," said Holmes coolly. "Please have a seat."

"I will do nothing of the kind," roared the man. "I followed my stepdaughter here. What

116

"Which of You Is Holmes?"

kind of nonsense has she been telling you?"

"My, the weather is a bit chilly," said Holmes, turning to Watson.

"What has she been telling you?" screamed the old man furiously.

"I hear, though, that the crocuses will bloom well," continued Holmes, ignoring the man.

"Ignore me, will you?" cried the doctor, taking a step toward Holmes, with his hunting crop raised. "I know you. You are Holmes, the meddler! Holmes, the busybody! Holmes, the Scotland Yard jack-in-the-box!"

Holmes chuckled. "Your speech is most amusing," he said. "When you leave, close the door, for I feel a draft."

"I'll go when I've had my say," cried Dr. Roylott. "Don't you dare meddle in my business! I am a dangerous man to oppose! See that you stay out of my business or I will do to you what I am about to do to your poker! Just watch." With that, he stepped forward, seized an iron poker from the fireplace, and

"Don't You Dare Meddle in My Business!"

bent it into a curve with his huge hands. Then he hurled the twisted poker into the fireplace and strode out of the room.

"He seems to be a very friendly person," said Holmes with a laugh. "I'm not as big as he, but if he had stayed, I might have shown him that my strength could match his."

And before Watson's amazed stare, Sherlock Holmes picked up the steel poker and straightened it out again. "How dare he degrade me by calling me part of Scotland Yard!" cried Holmes. "But I only hope that he will not punish Helen Stoner for having come here . . . . And now, Watson, as soon as we have had our breakfast, I have some business to attend to at the hall of official records."

It was nearly one o'clock when Sherlock Holmes returned from his errand. Watson saw in his hand a sheet of blue paper, scrawled all over with notes and figures.

Holmes explained, "I have seen the will of Dr. Roylott's late wife, and to determine the

Bending an Iron Poker

current value of her inheritance, I had to figure out the present worth of her investments. The yearly income to her family is about 750 pounds. Each daughter was to receive 250 pounds yearly upon her marriage."

"If that happened, the doctor would not have had much to live on," said Watson.

"Correct," said Holmes. "So through my morning's work, I proved that Dr. Roylott had very strong motives for preventing Julia's marriage, as well as Helen's now. And so, Watson, since the old man knows we are looking into his affairs, we dare not delay. I shall call a cab, and we shall be off to Waterloo station. Oh, and please do bring your revolver with you, Watson. It is always an excellent argument when one is up against a man who can twist steel pokers with his bare hands."

The train ride from Waterloo station to the village of Leatherhead was followed by one in a rented carriage through the blooming countryside, pleasantly scented by spring.

An Inheritance

After a four- or five-mile ride in silence, Holmes tapped Watson on the shoulder and pointed over a meadow. There, on a gentle slope, jutting out over a thick grove of trees, were the gray gables of an old mansion.

"Is that Stoke Moran?" Holmes asked the driver. "The house where the repair work is going on?"

"Yes, sir — the house of Dr. Grimesby Roylott," said the driver. "But I'd suggest you'd find it shorter going over this stile and following the footpath through the fields. The path is there, where the young lady is waiting."

Holmes shaded his eyes from the sun and looked where the driver was pointing. Helen Stoner was waiting there to meet them. Holmes and Watson got off, and the carriage rattled back toward Leatherhead.

"It's just as well that the driver thinks we're here on some repair business for the house," said Holmes. "We don't need him gossiping

Leaving the Carriage Near Stoke Moran

about our visit here."

Helen Stoner hurried forward to greet the two men, her face revealing her joy. "I have been waiting so eagerly for you," she cried. "Everything has worked out perfectly. Dr. Roylott has gone to town and won't be back before evening."

"We have already met the doctor," said Holmes, and he went on to tell Helen Stoner about her stepfather's visit that morning.

The woman turned white. "Good Heavens!" she cried. "He followed me. That man is so cunning, I never know when I am safe from him."

"Dr. Roylott is the one to be on guard," said Holmes, "for he shall soon find that someone more cunning than himself is on his trail. But all you need do, Miss Stoner, is lock yourself in your room tonight. If he gets violent, we shall take you to safety at your aunt's house. Now, we mustn't waste any time, so please take us to the house so we may examine the rooms."

Holmes Tries to Reassure Helen Stoner.

The big, moss-covered stone building had a high central portion and two curving wings. The left wing was in ruins, with the windows broken and boarded up. The central portion was in a little better condition, and the right wing was fairly modern, with blinds in the windows and smoke curling up the chimneys. This, then, was the wing where the family lived. Some scaffolding had been set up against one wall, and the stone had been broken into, but no workmen were there now.

Holmes walked up and down the neglected lawn and carefully examined the outsides of the windows. He stopped at the end window near the broken stone and asked Helen Stoner, "Is this your original room?"

"Yes, Mr. Holmes. And the one next to it was my sister's. The one closest to the main building is my stepfather's."

"Why have repairs been started in your bedroom?" asked Holmes. "There doesn't seem to be anything wrong with that wall."

Examining the End Window

"There isn't," answered Miss Stoner. "I believe it was an excuse to move me from my room."

"Ah! Maybe so," said Holmes. "Now, on the other side of this wing is the corridor that your bedroom doors open into, correct?"

"Yes."

"And does the corridor have windows?"

"Yes, very small ones — too small for anyone to fit through."

"So no one could get in from that side. Now, Miss Stoner, please go into your sister's room and bar the shutters so I might check them."

Helen Stoner did as Holmes asked, and as much as the detective tried, he could not force the shutters open. He then checked the hinges with his magnifying glass, but they were of solid iron and built into the stone. Finally, he stepped back and said, "No one could pass through these bolted shutters, so we'll now have to examine the rooms from the inside."

Helen Stoner led Holmes and Watson

Checking the Hinges

through a small side door into a whitewashed corridor onto which the three bedrooms opened. Holmes did not care to examine the end bedroom, but went immediately to the middle one — the one which Helen Stoner was now occupying and the one in which her sister had died.

It was a comfortable little room, with a low ceiling and a large fireplace. A brown chest of drawers stood in one corner, a narrow white bed in another, and a dressing table on the left side of the window. Two small wicker chairs and a small carpet in the center completed the furnishings in the room.

Holmes pulled one of the wicker chairs into a corner and sat staring around the room, studying every detail.

At last, he pointed to a thick bell-rope hanging beside the bed, its tassel resting on the pillow, and asked, "Where does that bell ring?"

"In the housekeeper's room," answered

Holmes Studies Every Detail of the Room.

Helen Stoner. "Why do you ask?"

"It looks newer than the other furnishings," remarked the detective.

"Yes, it was put there a couple of years ago, but my sister never used it. We always got what we wanted ourselves."

"Then it would seem an unnecessary expense," said Holmes.

Sherlock Holmes then turned his attention to the floors and walls. He crawled back and forth, examining the cracks between the floor boards, then did the same with the dark oak wall panels. Finally, he walked over to the bed, and stared at it and the wall behind it. He took the bell-rope in his hand and gave it a tug.

"It's a dummy!" he cried. "It's not even attached to a wire, so it can't possibly ring. It is only fastened to a hook above the opening for the air vent . . . . How strange!"

"I didn't even notice that," said Watson.

"Very strange!" muttered Holmes. "But there is another strange point in this room.

Tugging at the Bell-Rope

"Why would a builder open an air vent from one room into another room when he could have just as easily opened it to the outside air? Tell me, Miss Stoner, when was that air vent built into the wall?"

"About the same time as the bell-rope."

"That's what I suspected," said Holmes. "Most interesting changes — bell-ropes which don't ring a bell and ventilators which don't ventilate .... Now, Miss Stoner, I should like to see your stepfather's bedroom."

Dr. Grimesby Roylott's bedroom was larger than his stepdaughter's, but as simply furnished. Holmes walked around and carefully examined the camp-bed, a small wooden shelf of medical books, an armchair beside the bed, a wooden chair against the wall, a round table, and a large iron safe. "What's in here?" he asked, tapping the safe.

"My stepfather's business papers."

"Have you actually seen them inside?"

"Only once, some years ago."

An Air Vent from One Room to Another?

"Could there be a cat in it?" asked Holmes.

"What an absurd idea!" cried Helen Stoner.

"Not so," said Holmes, picking up a small saucer of milk from the top of the safe.

"We don't have a cat, Mr. Holmes, but my stepfather does keep a cheetah and a baboon."

"Well, that little saucer of milk could hardly satisfy a big cheetah," said Watson, as Holmes went on with his examination.

Holmes stopped in front of the wooden chair and examined its seat carefully with his magnifying glass. After several minutes, he rose. "Thank you," he said. "That is quite settled.... Hello! What's this?"

What had caught Holmes's eye was a small dog leash hung on one corner of the bed. It was curled and tied as if to make a noose.

Holmes fingered the leash and said coldly, "It's a wicked world, Watson, especially when a clever man turns his brains to crime." Then turning to Helen Stoner, Holmes continued, "I have seen enough, my dear lady. I shall now

"Could There Be a Cat in It?"

go out and walk on the lawn."

Watson and Helen Stoner followed Sherlock Holmes up and down the lawn several times before the detective broke the silence. "Miss Stoner, you must do exactly as I tell you, for your life may depend on it."

"I shall do whatever you tell me, Mr. Holmes."

"Then listen carefully. Your bedroom window faces the road and the village inn on the other side. Watson and I will be at the inn tonight. When your stepfather goes to bed, open your shutters and put your lamp in the window as a signal to us. Then you are to go into your old room and stay there for the night. Watson and I will then leave the inn and enter your room, where we shall spend the night and find out what is causing the strange noises."

Helen Stoner smiled. "Why, Mr. Holmes, I believe that you already know!"

"Perhaps I do," said Holmes with a smile.

"Watson and I Will Be at the Inn Tonight."

"But we must leave now, for if Dr. Roylott returned and found us here, all would be lost."

Holmes and Watson rented a front room on the upper floor at the Crown Inn. From their window they had a clear view of the bedroom wing of Stoke Moran manor house. Finally at dusk, they saw Dr. Grimesby Roylott drive through the gate, and enter the house.

As Holmes and Watson sat together in the darkness, Holmes said, "I have some doubts about taking you with me tonight, Watson. There is great danger."

"If you think I can be of help, then I shall certainly go along," answered Watson. "But what did you see in those rooms that makes you believe there will be danger?"

"I saw nothing unusual except the bell-rope and the ventilator," said Holmes. "But I knew we'd find a vent before we ever followed Helen Stoner to Stoke Moran."

"Holmes! How could you know?"

"My dear Watson, do you remember when

Watching from Their Room

Miss Stoner was telling us her story this morning, she said her sister smelled Dr. Roylott's Indian cigars. So, of course, I deducted that there had to be an opening between the two rooms. It had to be a small one or else the police would have noticed it."

"But is there anything suspicious about that?"

"Only the curious coincidences that a vent is built, a bell-cord is hung, and a lady who sleeps beneath them dies."

"I cannot see any connection," muttered Watson dejectedly.

"Did you notice anything strange about the bed?" asked Holmes.

"Why, no."

"It was clamped to the floor so it could not be moved. It would always have to be directly below the vent and the bell-cord, or call it the rope, for it was never meant to ring a bell."

"Holmes, I'm beginning to see what you're hinting at. I pray we are in time to prevent

Discussing Curious Coincidences

another horrible crime."

"I do too, Watson, for when a doctor becomes a criminal, he is the shrewdest kind, for he has both nerve and knowledge."

Holmes and Watson sat for several hours smoking their pipes and watching the house. Finally, about nine o'clock, the last of the lights went out, and all was dark.

They sat for two hours more, and just as their bedroom clock struck eleven, Holmes and Watson saw the glow of a single light from the middle bedroom at Stoke Moran.

"That's our signal," said Holmes, springing to his feet and grabbing his long, thin cane.

Moments later, the two men were out on the dark road, with a chilling wind blowing in their faces.

They had no difficulty entering the grounds of the old mansion, for the wall surrounding it was broken in many places. They made their way through the trees and across the lawn. As they were about to enter the opened window,

"That's Our Signal."

a hideous and distorted figure, almost like a child, darted out from behind a clump of bushes and ran swiftly across the lawn into the darkness.

For a moment, Holmes and Watson were startled. Then Holmes broke out into a low laugh and, putting his lips to Watson's ear, murmured, "That was the doctor's baboon, but he's gone now. We can go in."

The two men slipped off their shoes and proceeded into the bedroom. Holmes quietly closed the shutters, moved the lamp from the window onto a table, and looked around.

"We must be absolutely silent," Holmes whispered in Watson's ear. "We must sit without a light, or he'll see it through the vent."

Watson nodded.

"We must not sleep. Have your pistol ready. I will sit on the bed, and you sit in that chair."

Watson sat in the chair Holmes pointed to and laid his pistol silently on the table. Holmes placed his cane on the bed beside him. Next to

Startled by the Doctor's Baboon

it, he placed a box of matches and the stump of a candle. Then he turned down the lamp, and the room went black.

Holmes and Watson sat a few feet apart during their dreadful, silent vigil. Twelve o'clock struck, and one, then two, and three, and still the two men sat waiting.

Suddenly, a momentary gleam of light appeared at the ventilator, then vanished just as quickly, only to be replaced by a dim glow as if from a half-darkened lantern. Soon, a strong smell of burning oil and heated metal entered the room. A movement was heard from the next room, and then all was silent again. For half an hour, that silence continued and the smell got stronger.

Then another sound came from the doctor's room — a gentle sound, like steam escaping from a kettle. Upon hearing this, Holmes sprang from the bed, struck a match, and lashed out furiously with his cane at the bell pull.

A Dreadful, Silent Vigil!

"Do you see it, Watson?" he yelled, as he continued lashing.

"No, nothing," cried Watson. "The glare of your match blinded me for a moment, but I did hear a low, clear whistle."

Holmes stopped striking and, with a deadly pale face filled with horror, he stood gazing at the vent.

Suddenly, a horrible cry broke the silence — a cry that grew louder and louder, until it ended in a dreadful shriek of pain, fear, and anger. That cry struck Holmes and Watson dead in their tracks until its echo died away.

"What does it mean?" gasped Watson.

"It means that it is all over," Holmes answered. "Perhaps it is for the best. Take your pistol and we will enter Dr. Roylott's room."

Holmes lit the lamp and led the way down the corridor. He knocked at the doctor's bedroom door and, receiving no answer, he turned the handle and pushed open the door.

They stood in the doorway and looked

"Did You See It, Watson?"

around the room. On the table stood a lantern with its shutter half-open, throwing its light on the iron safe, whose door was open. Beside the table, on the wooden chair, sat Dr. Grimesby Roylott, dressed in a long dressing gown. His bare ankles stuck out beneath it, and his feet were thrust into red, backless Turkish slippers. Across his lap lay the long leash Holmes and Watson had seen earlier hanging on the bed.

The doctor's head was tilted upward, and his eyes were fixed in a dreadful stare at the ceiling. Around his head was wound a peculiar yellow band with brownish speckles.

"The band! The speckled band!" whispered Holmes.

Watson took a step forward. In an instant the strange headband began to move, and from the doctor's hair rose the squat, diamond-shaped head and puffed neck of a snake!

"It's a swamp adder!" cried Holmes. "The

"The Speckled Band!"

deadliest snake in India! Dr. Roylott must have died within ten seconds after he was bitten. Ah, the criminal has become the victim of the very crime he planned for another!"

As he spoke, Holmes grabbed the dog leash from the dead man's lap and threw the noose around the snake's neck. As the noose tightened, Holmes was able to pull the snake off the doctor's head and, carrying it at arm's length, threw it into the iron safe. Watson quickly closed the safe door after it.

Then, taking a deep sigh of relief, Watson turned to Holmes. "And now, Holmes, would you please fill me in on what I don't already know. How did you manage to solve this case in time to prevent another terrible crime?"

"At first, my dear Watson," began Holmes, "I came to a wrong conclusion. I, too, thought that Julia Stoner's dying words about a 'band' referred to the gypsies. But when I examined the mansion, I realized that whatever killed Julia Stoner and was now threatening her

Throwing a Noose Around the Snake's Neck

sister Helen could not have come from the outside.

"When I realized that the bell-pull was a dummy and then noticed the vent and saw the bed clamped to the floor, I suspected that the rope was used as a bridge — to pass something from the doctor's room, through the ventilator, and onto the bed. The idea of a snake instantly occurred to me, knowing that the doctor kept creatures from India as pets.

"The idea of using poison which would not show up in any chemical test would occur to a clever and ruthless man, especially one who had his medical training in the Far East. And then, it would take a sharp-eyed coroner to detect the two tiny punctures where the poisoned fangs did their work."

"But what was the whistle, Holmes?"

"The doctor had to get the snake back to his room, so he probably trained it, by use of the milk, to return at a signal — the whistle. He would put the snake through the vent, and

A Bridge Between Two Rooms

once through, it would crawl down the rope and land on the bed. Sooner or later it would attack its victim."

"And you came to these conclusions after examining Miss Stoner's room?" asked Watson in amazement.

"Yes," said Holmes. "I hadn't even seen the doctor's bedroom, but when I did, everything was confirmed. When I examined his chair, the very one in which he now sits, dead, I saw that he had been in the habit of standing on it — he would have to in order to reach the ventilator. The safe, the saucer of milk, and the noose of the dog leash erased any doubts."

"And the metallic clanging Miss Stoner heard?" asked Watson.

"Her stepfather closing the safe once he had the snake back inside."

"And when we waited in the darkness of Miss Stoner's room, what made you suddenly strike the match?"

"I heard the creature hiss, so I attacked it."

The Snake Crawled down the Rope.

"And that drove it back through the vent," added Watson.

"Yes, but the blows of my cane roused its temper, so that it attacked the first person it saw — *its own master!* In this way, I am probably responsible for Dr. Roylott's death, but I shall not be disturbed by it."

"Certainly not, Holmes," said Watson. "What you have done is not only to solve the mystery of the death of Julia Stoner, but to save the life of Helen Stoner as well."

With the mystery solved, Holmes and Watson broke the news of her stepfather's death to the terrified Helen Stoner, then took her to her aunt's house on the morning train.

Once the police were notified, an official inquiry was made. The conclusion was that the doctor had been accidentally killed while playing with his dangerous pet.

As Holmes and Watson traveled back to London on the train the next day, Watson looked troubled.

"It Attacked . . . Its Own Master!"

"What's bothering you, old chap?" asked Holmes.

" I cannot understand why you didn't inform the police of Dr. Roylott's crime and the real truth as to how he died."

"My dear Watson," said Holmes, "I felt that Helen Stoner had been through enough tragedy in her life, and to expose her stepfather for the murderer he was would only extend her grief. This way, she can begin a new, happy life with her future husband without the shame and scandal that would have followed her if the truth were known. And besides, the local police would have been most embarrassed had I revealed that the great Sherlock Holmes had solved a crime which they had blundered."

"Yes, indeed!" agreed Watson. "You *are* the great Sherlock Holmes!"

"You *Are* the Great Sherlock Holmes!"

Holmes Studies the Classified Columns.

The Adventure of the Copper Beeches

It was a cold spring morning, and Sherlock Holmes and Dr. Watson were sitting on either side of a cheery fire in the sitting-room of 221B Baker Street. A thick fog made the houses outside look like dark, shapeless blurs.

The gas lamp was lit, and by its light, Holmes was studying the classified advertisement columns of various newspapers. Finally, having given up his search, he threw the last paper down and sat back, smoking his long pipe and gazing into the fire.

"I fear, Watson," he said glumly, "that my

practice has come down to finding lost lead pencils and giving advice to young ladies from boarding schools. I think that I have hit bottom at last with this note I received from a boarding school this morning." Holmes took a crumpled letter from the pocket of his dressing-gown and tossed it across to Watson.

"It is dated last night," said Watson, "and it reads: 'I AM VERY ANXIOUS TO ASK YOUR ADVICE AS TO WHETHER OR NOT I SHOULD ACCEPT A POSITION OFFERED TO ME AS GOVERNESS. I SHALL CALL AT 10:30 TOMORROW MORNING IF THAT IS CONVENIENT FOR YOU.' And it is signed 'VIOLET HUNTER.' Do you know the young lady, Holmes?"

"Certainly not!" exclaimed Holmes. "But since it is 10:30 now, I would assume that the footsteps I hear in the hallway are Miss Hunter's."

Just then the door opened, and a plain but neatly dressed young lady entered the room.

"I Have Hit Bottom with This Note."

She had a bright-looking face covered with freckles, and she walked with the self-assurance of a woman who is accustomed to making her own way in the world.

As Holmes and Watson rose to greet her, Violet Hunter spoke. "Please excuse my troubling you, Mr. Holmes, but since I've had a very strange experience and since I have no parents or family from whom to seek advice, I thought of coming to you."

"Do sit down, Miss Hunter, and tell Dr. Watson and me your story," said Holmes, who seemed impressed with the young woman.

"For the past five years, I have been a governess to the child of Colonel Spence Munro," explained Miss Hunter. "But two months ago, the colonel was transferred to a post in Canada. Although I have been trying to find another position during this time, I have not been successful. What little money I had saved began to run out."

"Have you answered classified ads for any

Violet Hunter Comes for Advice.

governess positions?" asked Watson.

"Answered them and placed several myself, sir," said Miss Hunter, "but with no success."

"And have you tried employment agencies?" asked Holmes.

"Yes, Mr. Holmes. Miss Staper's Agency is quite well known for specializing in governess positions, and I have been checking with them every week. When I stopped in last week, I was shown into Miss Staper's offfce. A rather stout, smiling man was seated next to her desk. As I entered and he saw me, he turned in his chair with a start.

" 'She will do!' he cried to Miss Staper. Perfect! I couldn't ask for anything better.' Then he turned to me and asked, 'Are you looking for a position as a governess, miss?'

" 'Yes, sir,' I replied.

" 'And what salary are you asking?'

" 'I earned four pounds a month at my last job, sir,' I told him.

" 'Tut! Tut! A mere nothing!' he cried. 'For

At Miss Staper's Agency

such an attractive young lady, I would not think of paying you less than 100 pounds a year.'

"You may imagine, Mr. Holmes, that poor as I was, such an offer seemed too good to be true, but when the gentleman saw the doubt on my face, he immediately offered to pay me half my first year's salary in advance. How thoughtful it was, especially since I had many debts to pay. Yet, something seemed strange about this whole situation, and I felt I needed to know more before I gave him an answer. So I began by asking where he lived.

" 'In Hampshire,' he replied. 'A charming country house called the Copper Beeches.'

" 'And my duties, sir?' I asked.

" 'One child — one dear little lad of six,' he said with a laugh. 'Quite skillful at killing cockroaches with a slipper. Smack! Smack! Smack! And three gone in a wink!'

"I was a bit startled, Mr. Holmes, at the boy's idea of fun, but I assumed that the father

The Copper Beeches

was joking. I then asked if there were any other requirements or duties.

" 'Only to obey any little orders my wife might give — nothing out of the ordinary,' he said, then added, 'but would you object to wearing any dress we might give you — just a little whim of ours?'

" 'No, sir,' I replied, rather surprised.

" 'And if we asked you to sit in a certain chair, would you be agreeable?'

" 'Certainly, sir,' I replied, but my amazement was increasing.

" 'And would you cut your hair short?'

"I could hardly believe my ears, Mr. Holmes. As you can see, I have long, thick, luxuriant hair, of which I have always been quite proud. I couldn't dream of sacrificing it to suit someone's whim. So to this request, I replied, 'I'm afraid that is quite impossible.'

"His smiling face darkened and he said, 'I'm afraid it will be necessary. It is a little fancy of my wife's. Are you certain you won't?'

"Would You Cut Your Hair Short?"

" 'I really cannot,' I answered firmly.

"At that point, Miss Staper looked at me with annoyance. She was understandably upset at losing a good commission. 'Well, Miss Hunter,' she finally sputtered, 'it seems useless for us to keep you on our register, since you are refusing such an excellent offer.'

"Well, Mr. Holmes, when I returned home to my small room, with little food in the cupboard and several unpaid bills on the table, I began to wonder if I hadn't been foolish. These people might be eccentric, but they were willing to pay for this eccentricity. Besides, my hair might look becoming short. I thought this way for three days, and was at the point of returning to the agency to see if the position was still available when I received this letter from the gentleman himself."

Sherlock Holmes took the letter Violet Hunter handed to him and began to read:

"THE COPPER BEECHES, WINCHESTER. DEAR MISS HUNTER —

Remembering Unpaid Bills

THE ADVENTURE OF THE COPPER BEECHES

MY WIFE WAS VERY IMPRESSED WITH MY DESCRIPTION OF YOU AND IS ANXIOUS FOR YOU TO COME. WE ARE WILLING TO INCREASE OUR OFFER TO 120 POUNDS A YEAR, SO AS TO PAY YOU FOR ANY INCONVENIENCE OUR LITTLE FANCIES MAY CAUSE YOU.

MY WIFE IS QUITE FOND OF A SHADE OF BLUE CALLED ELECTRIC BLUE AND WOULD LIKE YOU TO WEAR A DRESS OF THAT COLOR IN THE MORNINGS. YOU NEED NOT GO TO THE EXPENSE OF BUYING ONE, AS WE HAVE ONE HERE BELONGING TO MY DAUGHTER ALICE, WHO NOW LIVES IN PHILADELPHIA, IN THE U.S.A. IT WILL FIT YOU QUITE WELL.

HOWEVER, I MUST REMAIN QUITE FIRM UPON THE POINT OF CUTTING YOUR HAIR. I AM AWARE OF ITS BEAUTY, BUT I HOPE THAT YOUR INCREASE IN SALARY WILL MAKE UP FOR ITS LOSS.

YOURS FAITHFULLY, JEPHRO RUCASTLE."

When he had finished reading, Sherlock Holmes returned the letter to Violet Hunter

Holmes Reads Jephro Rucastle's Letter.

and sat back in his chair. "And what have you decided to do?" he asked.

"I decided to accept the position, but before I inform Mr. Rucastle of my decision, I would like your opinion of what these strange conditions could possibly mean. Do you think Mr. Rucastle's wife is a lunatic and he simply wishes to humor her fancies?"

"It is possible," said Holmes. "In any case, this is not a position which I would permit my own sister to apply for."

"But the money, Mr. Holmes! "

"Yes, the pay is good — *too* good, I fear. Why should they give you 120 pounds a year when they could get any of the finest governesses in England for 40 pounds? Yes, there is some strange and mysterious reason behind that."

"Exactly, Mr. Holmes!" cried Miss Hunter. "And that is why I've come to you. I wanted you to know everything, so that if I needed your help while I was at Mr. Rucastle's . . . ."

"The Pay is Good—*Too* Good, I Fear."

"By all means, Miss Hunter," said Holmes. "If you should find yourself in danger, be it day or night, a telegram would bring me to your help immediately."

"You have eased my mind considerably, Mr. Holmes," said Violet Hunter, as she rose from her chair, smiling. "Now I shall sacrifice my poor hair tonight and leave for Winchester tomorrow. Good night, Mr. Holmes, Dr. Watson, and thank you both."

As Violet Hunter shut the door behind her, Watson turned to Holmes, saying, "Violet Hunter seems to be a fine young lady who is well able to take care of herself."

"She will need to," said Holmes, with a worried look on his face. "If I'm not mistaken, we will hear from her before many days pass."

During the next two weeks, Sherlock Holmes sat for many hours with that same worried look on his face. Finally, late one night, the expected telegram arrived.

"Watson!" cried Holmes after reading the

The Expected Telegram

message. "We must leave for Winchester tomorrow. Miss Hunter pleads with us to meet her at noon at the Black Swan Inn. She fears she is at her wits' end."

Sherlock Holmes and Dr. Watson boarded the 9:30 train from London for the two-hour ride to Winchester. Watson was enthused at the countryside on a beautiful spring day, but Holmes was not impressed by its beauty.

"No, Watson," he said, "I cannot see the beauty. I look at the countryside and think how scattered the farmhouses are and how easily a crime committed there would go unnoticed. I fear for Violet Hunter's safety."

"But she must be free to come and go," said Watson, "since she is meeting us in Winchester. She is obviously not being personally threatened."

"True," said Holmes, "but I still fear danger."

When Sherlock Holmes and Dr. Watson arrived at the Black Swan Inn, Violet Hunter

The Train Ride to Winchester

was already there. She had rented a sitting-room and had ordered lunch for the three of them.

"I am delighted that you both came," she said eagerly. "I need your advice."

"What has happened to you?" asked Holmes.

"I will tell you, but I must be quick. I promised Mr. Rucastle to be back before three o'clock."

"Then tell us everything as it happened," said Holmes, as they sat down to lunch in the sitting-room.

"To begin, Mr. Holmes, I have not had any actual bad treatment from Mr. and Mrs. Rucastle, but I cannot understand them and the reasons for their behavior.

"When I arrived here two weeks ago, Mr. Rucastle met me with his cart and drove me to the Copper Beeches, which is named for the clump of copper beech trees at the front door. I was introduced to Mrs. Rucastle and the

"Tell Us Everything As It Happened."

child, Edward. I soon discovered that the concerns for Mrs. Rucastle's sanity, which we discussed two weeks ago in London, were unfounded. She is not mad, only a silent, pale woman, much younger than her husband. I take him for about forty-five and her, about thirty. They have been married seven years. He had been a widower, he told me, and his only child, a 20-year-old daughter, had gone to Philadelphia because she did not get along with her young stepmother."

"Tell me more about Mrs. Rucastle," said Holmes.

"She's a rather colorless person, but passionately devoted to her husband and their little son. She seemed to have some secret sorrow, though, and I often see her deep in thought, with the saddest look on her face. More than once I found her in tears. I thought perhaps it might be because of her son, for never have I met such a spoiled and bad-tempered little creature. He divides his time

A Spoiled Little Creature

between savage anger and gloomy sulking. His one amusement is to inflict pain on any creature weaker than himself, like capturing mice, birds, or insects. But he has little to do with my story, Mr. Holmes."

"Not so," said Sherlock Holmes. "All these details are important, whether they seem so to you or not."

"The only unpleasant thing about the house is the two servants — a man and his wife. Toller is a rough, uncouth man with a constant smell of liquor on him. I've seen him drunk twice in these last two weeks, but Mr. Rucastle seems to overlook it. Mrs. Toller is a tall, strong woman with a sour face. They are unpleasant, but devoted to the Rucastles."

"Well, Miss Hunter," said Holmes, "so far, nothing is *that* out of the ordinary."

"Nothing was, Mr. Holmes," said Miss Hunter, "... for the first two days. But on the morning of the third day, Mrs. Rucastle whispered something to her husband at the break-

Mr. and Mrs. Toller—the Servants

fast table. Both of them looked at me as I sat there puzzled. Then Mr. Rucastle spoke.

" 'My wife and I are pleased that you agreed to indulge our whim by cutting your hair, Miss Hunter. Now we wish you to wear that electric blue dress I spoke to you about. You will find it laid out on your bed.'

"Well, I went up to my room, Mr. Holmes, and the dress I found waiting was of a peculiar shade of blue — of excellent material, but definitely worn before. However, it fit as perfectly as if it had been made for me. I put it on, and when I joined Mr. and Mrs. Rucastle in the drawing-room, both were delighted with my appearance.

"Mr. Rucastle motioned me to a chair, which had been placed close to the middle of three large windows overlooking the front of the house. As I sat with my back to the window, Mr. Rucastle began to walk up and down on the other side of the room, all the while telling me some of the funniest stories I have ever

The Blue Dress Was On the Bed.

heard. I laughed until I was quite weary.

"Mrs. Rucastle, however, who evidently has no sense of humor, sat with a sad, anxious face and never once smiled. Finally, after an hour Mr. Rucastle ceased, then told me I might change my clothes and attend to my duties with little Edward in the nursery."

"Was this the only time such an incident occured?" asked Holmes.

"No, Mr. Holmes. Two days later, the same performance took place. This time, after I had been laughing at Mr. Rucastle's funny stories for nearly an hour, he handed me a book and after moving my chair sideways, so my shadow wouldn't fall upon the page, he asked me to read to him. I read for about ten minutes, and suddenly, in the middle of a sentence, he ordered me to stop, change my dress, and return to my duties."

"Is that the entire story?" asked Dr. Watson.

"No, sir. As the days went on, I became

Laughing at Mr. Rucastle's Funny Stories

more and more curious about these unusual performances. Mr. Rucastle was always so careful to turn my face *away* from the window that I started having the wildest desires to see behind me.

"At first, it seemed impossible, but I soon came up with an idea. My hand mirror had broken during my trip to the Copper Beeches, so I now hid a piece of glass in my handkerchief. During Mr. Rucastle's next performance, my laughter brought tears to my eyes so I had the opportunity to bring my handkerchief up to my face. I must confess, Mr. Holmes, that I was somewhat disappointed. All I saw was a man standing in the road, looking in my direction. He was a small, bearded man, in a gray suit. I lowered my handkerchief and saw Mrs. Rucastle staring at me intently. I am certain that she guessed I had a mirror in my hand, for she rose at once and informed her husband that someone in the road was staring at me.

Looking into a Hidden Mirror

" 'A friend of yours, Miss Hunter?' Mr. Rucastle asked me.

" 'No, sir,' I replied. 'I know no one in or around Winchester.'

" 'Then kindly motion for him to go away.'

" 'But, sir,' I protested, 'wouldn't it be better to ignore him?'

" 'No, no! Otherwise he'll be loitering around here all the time. Now, please, Miss Hunter, turn around and wave him away.'

"I did as I was told, Mr. Holmes. Then Mr. Rucastle immediately closed the drapes. That was a few days ago, and from that day on, I have not sat in the window, nor worn the blue dress, nor seen the man in the road."

"Your story is most interesting, Miss Hunter," said Holmes. "Please continue."

"On the very first day that I was at the Copper Beeches, Mr. Rucastle took me to a small shed near the kitchen door. As we approached it, I heard the rattling of a chain and the sound of a large animal moving about.

Closing the Drapes

"Pointing to a slit between two planks, Mr. Rucastle said, 'Look through here, Miss Hunter. Isn't he a beauty!'

"I looked through the slit and saw two glowing eyes and a shadowy figure huddled in the darkness.

" 'Don't be frightened,' said Mr. Rucastle, laughing. 'It's only Carlo, my mastiff. Toller feeds him only once a day and lets him loose every night on the grounds. God help the trespasser that guard dog gets his fangs into!' He warned me not to go out at night either."

"Strange that your employer should need to guard his grounds in such a violent manner," commented Dr. Watson.

"Yes, Dr. Watson," agreed Violet Hunter, "and it was chilling to see that huge animal walking across the lawn at night."

"Has anything else happened that might be considered unusual?" asked Holmes.

"I was just coming to that, Mr. Holmes. As you know, I had cut off my hair in London. It

Showing Off His Mastiff Guard Dog

was in a large curl, and I kept it. It was in the bottom of my trunk. Well, one evening after young Edward was in bed, I began to examine the furniture in my room. There was an old three-drawer chest. The two top drawers had been open when I arrived, so I put my things in them. But the bottom drawer was locked.

"On this particular evening, I was trying to decide where to put the things I hadn't yet unpacked, when I realized that I didn't have the use of that third drawer. Thinking it had been locked by mistake, I took out my bunch of keys for the house and found one that fit. When I opened the drawer, I found ... my curl of hair!

"I took it out and examined it — the same color, the same thickness. 'But how can it be,' I asked myself. 'How can my hair be locked in the drawer?' My hands trembled as I opened my trunk and tossed out what few clothes remained in it. And there, from the bottom, I drew out my own curl of hair!

Two Curls of Hair——Exactly Alike!

"I placed mine next to the one I had found in the drawer and found them to be identical. Naturally, this puzzled me greatly, but I did not mention it to the Rucastles, since I really had no right opening a locked drawer."

"That certainly *is* puzzling," said Holmes. "Now, is that all Watson and I should know?"

"Just one more thing, Mr. Holmes. There is one wing of the house which appeared to be uninhabited. The door of the Tollers' rooms faced the door to this wing, but this door was always locked. One day, however, as I reached the top of the stairs, I saw Mr. Rucastle coming out of this door, his keys in his hand. But his face, which I had always seen smiling and pleasant, now was red and crinkled in anger with veins standing out at his temples as if ready to burst. He locked the door and hurried past me without a word or a look."

"Aha, Miss Hunter," said Dr. Watson, smiling, "so I'm sure that with your curiosity and fine powers of observation, you found the

A Door That Was Always Locked

answer to this mystery."

"I'm afraid not, Dr. Watson. In fact, I have become *more* curious . . . and even terrified!"

"How so?" asked Holmes.

"The following day, I took Edward for a stroll around the part of the grounds from which I could see that wing. Four windows looked out; three were simply dirty, but the fourth was shuttered up. As I strolled along, glancing up at the windows from time to time, Mr. Rucastle came out, looking just as smiling and jovial as ever.

" 'You seem to be curious about this wing, Miss Hunter,' he said. 'I use it for my hobby — photography. That shuttered window is my darkroom.' He spoke gaily, but his eyes showed suspicion and annoyance. At that moment, I realized that those rooms contained some secret which I was not supposed to know, and my curiosity then made me want to discover what that secret was."

"And did you discover the secret, Miss

Glancing Up at a Shuttered Window

Hunter?" asked Holmes.

"No, Mr. Holmes, and because I fear there is something evil going on there, I came to you."

"Evil?" cried Dr. Watson. "How so?"

"At first it was only my woman's instinct. But then yesterday, my fears became very real. Besides Mr. Rucastle, I have seen both Toller and his wife going in and out of those deserted rooms. Once, I saw Toller carrying a large black cloth bag into the room with him. Toller drinks a great deal and last night he was very drunk.

"When I came upstairs, I saw that the key had been left in the door, no doubt by Toller. Mr. and Mrs. Rucastle and the Tollers were all downstairs, so I had the perfect opportunity to sneak in. I turned the key quietly in the lock and slipped inside. I found myself in a hallway facing three doors in a row. The first and third were open, and revealed dusty, empty rooms. The middle door was closed and barred with an iron bar, padlocked to a ring in the wall.

A Barred and Padlocked Door!

This door led to the room with the shuttered window. Yet despite the shutters blocking off the light, a glimmer shone beneath the door, probably from a skylight, I thought.

"As I stood in the hall, gazing at the sinister door, I suddenly heard footsteps from inside the room. Terror seized me, Mr. Holmes, and I turned and ran...straight into the arms of Mr. Rucastle, standing in the doorway.

" 'So, it was you,' he said, smiling.

" 'Oh, Mr. Rucastle, I'm so frightened,' I gasped.

" 'What frightened you?' he asked, smiling. But his voice was so soothing that I was immediately on guard.

" 'I was foolish to go into that wing, sir, but the eerie stillness in there frightened me so badly that I ran out.'

" 'Only that?' he asked. 'Now do you see why I lock that door, my dear young lady? It is to keep out people who have no business there.' He was still smiling as he went on, 'Well, now

"I Ran into the Arms of Mr. Rucastle."

that you know, you will never cross that threshold again.' And in an instant, his smile turned to the glare of a demon as he said, 'For if you do, I'll throw you to the mastiff!' "

"Good heavens!" cried Watson.

"I was so terrified," continued Miss Hunter, "that I don't know what I did. I must have rushed by him to my room, for the next thing I remember I was lying on my bed, trembling all over. And then I thought of you, Mr. Holmes. Of course, I might have run away, but my curiosity was almost as strong as my fears, so I went down to the telegraph office, which is less than half a mile from the house, and sent you the wire.

"I had no difficulty getting the time off to come into Winchester this morning, but I must be back by three o'clock, for Mr. and Mrs. Rucastle are going out for the afternoon and evening, and I must look after Edward. Now, Mr. Holmes, can you tell me what this all means and what I should do?"

"I'll Throw You to the Mastiff!"

Sherlock Holmes rose and paced up and down the room, one hand in his pocket and a serious look on his face. Suddenly, he stopped and faced Violet Hunter. "Is Toller still drunk?" he asked.

"Yes. I heard his wife tell Mrs. Rucastle that she couldn't do anything with him."

"Good!" cried Holmes. "And the Rucastles will be out tonight?"

"Yes."

"And is there a cellar with a good, sturdy lock?"

"Yes, the wine-cellar."

"Fine, fine. Now, Miss Hunter, I must ask one more thing of you, and I ask it only because you are a brave and sensible woman."

"Anything, Mr. Holmes."

"Watson and I shall be at the Copper Beeches by seven o'clock tonight. With the Rucastles out and Toller drunk, that leaves only Mrs. Toller to worry about. Can you send her down into the cellar on an errand and then

Holmes Paces Up and Down the Room.

lock her in once she's down there?"

"Certainly, Mr. Holmes."

"Excellent! That will give us the opportunity to look into this affair thoroughly. Of course, it is obvious that you were brought to the Copper Beeches to impersonate someone, and that someone is a prisoner in the deserted wing of the house."

"But who is that?" asked Watson.

"I'm certain that it is Mr. Rucastle's daughter Alice, who was supposed to be in America, Watson," answered Holmes. "I am certain that Miss Hunter was chosen for the job because of her strong resemblance to Alice Rucastle — only the hair length was different, and that was solved by having Miss Hunter cut hers off. And the man Miss Hunter saw in the road was probably a friend of Alice Rucastle's — possibly her fiance. Your little impersonation was undoubtedly designed to show the gentleman that Miss Rucastle was perfectly happy without him."

A Mysterious Impersonation?

"And the dog prevents this fellow from contacting Miss Rucastle at night," added Watson.

"Oh, I am sure you are right, Mr. Holmes, and you too, Dr. Watson," cried Violet Hunter. "Oh, let us not lose a moment in helping this poor creature."

"We must be cautious," said Holmes, "for we are dealing with a cruel and cunning man. We can do nothing until seven o'clock, and then we will solve the mystery."

At a few minutes before seven that evening, Sherlock Holmes and Dr. Watson left their carriage at a nearby inn and proceeded on foot to the Copper Beeches. Violet Hunter was standing on the doorstep, smiling.

"Did you do it?" asked Holmes.

A loud thudding noise came from somewhere downstairs. "That is Mrs. Toller in the cellar," said Violet Hunter. "Her husband is snoring on the kitchen floor, but I managed to lift his keys."

Greeting Homes and Watson with the Keys

"You have done very well!" cried Holmes. "Now lead us upstairs and we shall put an end to this ugly business."

Violet Hunter led Holmes and Watson up the stairs and unlocked the door to the deserted wing. Within moments, they were facing the barred door Violet Hunter had described earlier. Holmes found the key to open the padlock and removed the bar. Then he tried the other keys in the door lock, but none fit.

"Surely whoever is inside must have heard us," said Watson.

The silence from inside the room brought a frown to the detective's face. "I hope we are not too late," he said. "Watson, we'll have to break down the door."

With Holmes and Watson heaving their shoulders against it, the door gave way. They rushed into the room ... but it was empty! There was only a small, rough bed and a little table. The skylight above was open, and the

An Empty Room and an Open Skylight!

prisoner was gone!

"I fear that this villain Rucastle has guessed Miss Hunter's plans and has carried off his victim," said Holmes.

"But how?" cried Watson.

"Through the skylight," said Holmes, and he swung himself up onto the roof. "I see how, Watson," he called down. "There's a long ladder up against the eaves of the house."

"But that's impossible!" cried Miss Hunter. "The ladder wasn't there when the Rucastles left."

"Then Mr. Rucastle came back and put it there. He's a clever and dangerous man," said Holmes, as he jumped back down into the room. "And if the footsteps I now hear on the stairs are his, we had better have our pistols ready."

At that moment, Mr. Rucastle appeared at the door, a heavy stick in his hand. Violet Hunter screamed and drew back against the wall, but Sherlock Holmes jumped in front of

Holmes Checks the Roof.

the evil-looking man.

"You villain!" cried Holmes. "What have you done with your daughter? Where is she?"

Mr. Rucastle's bulging eyes surveyed the room and then stopped at the skylight. "I'd better ask you that," he shrieked. "Spies! Thieves! I've caught you, but you shall not escape!" And he turned and fled down the stairs.

"He's gone for the dog!" screamed Violet Hunter.

Holmes, Watson, and Violet Hunter rushed down the stairs. Just as they reached the hall, they heard the horrible baying of the hound, followed by a scream of agony.

At that moment, an elderly man, with a red, puffy face and shaking knees, staggered into the hall from the kitchen. It was Toller. "My God!" he cried. "Someone has let the dog loose. And he hasn't been fed in two days. Quick, quick, or it'll be too late!"

Holmes, Watson, and Toller rushed out onto

"Spies! Thieves! I've Caught You!"

the grounds. There, near the dump of Copper Beeches, was the huge, famished hound, its jaws buried in Mr. Rucastle's throat, while the man screamed and writhed in agony.

Watson aimed quickly and shot. The huge dog fell dead. Holmes and Toller carried Mr. Rucastle, living but badly mangled, into the house and laid him on the sofa. Dr. Watson and Violet Hunter did what they could to relieve the pain. As the four stood around the sofa, a tall, thin woman entered the room.

"Mrs. Toller!" cried Violet Hunter.

"Yes, miss. Mr. Rucastle let me out when he came back before he went upstairs. Ah, miss, it is a pity you didn't tell me what you were planning, for I could have saved you the trouble."

"Aha!" cried Holmes, "Then you know everything about this affair, Mrs. Toller."

"Yes, sir, I do, and I am ready to tell you what I know," said the housekeeper.

"Then please sit down and let us hear it, for

"You Know Everything About This Affair."

there are some points that still puzzle me."

"Please, remember, sir," began Mrs. Toller, "that if there's any police or court business, I told you everything. Truly I would have done it sooner if I hadn't been locked in the cellar. I'm your friend, just as I was Miss Alice's."

"Of course, Mrs. Toller," said Holmes gently. "Now please tell us what you know about Alice Rucastle."

The old woman began her story. "From the time her father married again, Miss Alice was never happy at home. She was ignored completely and had no say in anything. But it got even worse after she met Mr. Fowler."

"That is the young man who became interested in her?" asked Holmes.

"Yes, sir, a real fine young man — a seaman she met at a friend's house."

"Tell me, Mrs. Toller, was Miss Rucastle a wealthy young lady?" asked Holmes.

"She had a large income from her dear mother's will, but being as sweet and innocent

Mrs. Toller Tells of Alice's Unhappiness.

as she was, Miss Alice just left everything in Mr. Rucastle's hands. He knew she would never question what he did with her money. But if Miss Alice married, Mr. Rucastle knew that her husband would be entitled to share that money with her."

"I see," said Holmes. "That forced his hand, I suppose."

"Yes, sir. Mr. Rucastle tried to get Miss Alice to sign a paper letting him use her money whether she married or not, but she refused. Then Mr. Rucastle kept at her constantly for weeks and weeks until she took sick. The fever nearly killed her, and for six weeks we didn't know if she would pull through. Because of the fever, all her beautiful hair had to be cut off. But she recovered — even though her illness left her pale and thin."

"And what of Mr. Fowler through all this?" asked Holmes.

"He stuck by her, as true as a man could be."

Alice Refused to Sign the Papers.

"Thank you, Mrs. Toller," said Holmes. "I think I can now figure out the rest. Mr. Rucastle then imprisoned his daughter in the deserted wing of the house and told Mr. Fowler that she no longer cared to see him."

"Yes, sir. But Mr. Fowler persisted in coming around and watching the house, hoping to see Miss Alice."

"So Mr. Rucastle brought Miss Hunter down from London to impersonate Alice and try to persuade Mr. Fowler that she was no longer interested in him."

"That was it, sir."

"And I presume, Mrs. Toller," continued Holmes, "that Mr. Fowler managed to intercept you, on your way to the market perhaps, and persuaded you with pleas or maybe money to help him."

"Mr. Fowler was a very kind and generous gentleman," said Mrs. Toller with a smile.

"And he sent over a good supply of whiskey for your husband to get him drunk while you

Persuading Mrs. Toller To Help

made certain that a ladder was ready for him, as soon as the Rucastles left the house."

"That's just the way it happened, sir."

"Thank you, Mrs. Toller. You have certainly cleared up everything that was puzzling us. And now, I hear voices in the hall. It's probably your husband with Mrs. Rucastle and the doctor. So, Watson, I think we'd best escort Miss Hunter back to Winchester and get out of here ourselves, for the Rucastles will feel that we have no business being here."

"Right, Holmes," said Dr. Watson. "But may I congratulate you again on a brilliant solution. You had guessed everything even before Mrs. Toller explained it."

"Simple observation and deduction, my dear Watson," said Holmes, smiling.

Some weeks later, while Holmes and Watson were seated before the fire at 221B Baker Street, the good doctor brought up the case one last time.

"Holmes," he said, "have you had any further

Mrs. Toller Got the Ladder Ready.

news about the Copper Beeches?"

"Yes, Watson. I've learned that Mr. Rucastle survived that attack by the hound, but he is a defeated man, kept alive only by the care of his devoted wife and loyal servants."

"And what of his daughter?"

"Miss Alice Rucastle and Mr. Fowler were married in Southampton the day after they ran away from the Copper Beeches. They are now living on the Island of Mauritius, a British colony in the Indian Ocean. The young man holds a government job there."

"And Miss Violet Hunter?"

"Her letter says she has found a fine position as the head of a private school in Walsall, and is quite happy with it."

"Then all is well, Holmes," said Watson with a contented sigh.

"No, Watson," said Holmes glumly, "not quite. Nothing will be well until there is another mystery to challenge the talents of the great Sherlock Holmes!"

Good News in Violet Hunter's Letter